Presents

T0316287

Crooked Wood

By Gillian Plowman

Based on the television film **Number 27** by Michael Palin
First shown on the BBC, 23rd October 1988

This version of *Crooked Wood* was first produced at
Jermyn Street Theatre on 9 September 2008

This production is dedicated to the memory of
Judy Campbell and Dan Crawford

JUDY CAMPBELL

Judy Campbell will probably be best remembered for her evocative and husky-voiced rendition of Eric Maschwitz's romantic song *A Nightingale Sang in Berkeley Square* which captivated audiences of a war-torn London. It was the song that changed her life. Noël Coward was in the audience on the first night and went backstage to congratulate the unknown young actress. 'It takes talent to put over a song when you haven't got a voice,' he told her; 'one day we will act together'. He was as good as his word. They toured the provinces, Judy creating the roles of Joanna in *Present Laughter*, Ethel in *This Happy Breed* and playing Elvira in *Blithe Spirit*. She also appeared with him in twice-weekly troop concerts before returning to the West End with *Present Laughter* and *This Happy Breed*.

After six decades in leading roles on the West End stage Judy made her National Theatre debut in 2002 playing Grandmere, 'a compellingly spectral, lace gowned presence' in Harold Pinter's adaptation of Proust's *Remembrance of Things Past.* A side of Judy Campbell that is perhaps less well known is that she was a writer of some talent: one of her plays, *The Bright One*, was produced in the West End, directed by Rex Harrison, with Kay Kendall in the leading role. Judy always took a keen interest in new plays and when in 2003 Dan Crawford told her about *The Crooked Wood* she was extremely enthusiastic about performing in it and made valuable contributions to the script. In 2003, at the end of a 67-year career as an actress of elegant distinction she gave her farewell London performances at Jermyn Street Theatre with *Where Are the Songs We Sung?*, a nostalgic garland of scenes from plays, songs and memories. The evening recalled Judy's Grantham childhood with her mother the actress Mary Fulton and her father, a playwright, actor and manager of the Theatre Royal, J A Campbell. It recounted the 1950s with Sandy Wilson, by way of the Liverpool rep' with Robert Helpmann, the wintry tours and troop concerts with Noël Coward and cheering up West End punters during the Blitz on London and – to a standing ovation every night – she again performed *A Nightingale Sang in Berkeley Square.*

After her death in 2004 her name was commemorated on the actresses' dressing room door at the Jermyn Street Theatre.

DAN CRAWFORD

Dan Crawford was born in Hackensack, New Jersey, and began his theatrical life in Robert Ludlum's theatre in a shopping mall at the age of seventeen. Ten years later, in 1970, he founded the King's Head Theatre in London, the first pub theatre since Shakespearean times and the first dinner theatre in the UK. In the early 1990s he came across Michael Palin's television film *Number 27* and asked permission to adapt it for the stage. Permission duly granted, he commissioned Gillian Plowman to adapt and he directed the piece with great success at the King's Head. Some years later, wanting to develop it further, and working closely with Gillian Plowman, he contacted Penny Horner at Jermyn Street Theatre to co-mount a second production. Dan died in 2005 leaving a legacy of 35 years of award winning theatre, 38 transfers to the West End and Broadway and the discovery of many household names, including Hugh Grant and Victoria Wood, and the championing of the early work of Tom Stoppard, Steven Berkoff, Stewart Parker, Athol Fugard and many others. His sensitivity to the creative elements of production, his direction, the King's Head and the countless people he mentored and inspired are his legacy. He is survived by his wife and daughter, Stephanie and Katey, who have kept the King's Head going for him against all odds, his brother Michael and his indomitable mother Edna from whom he inherited his incredible zest for life. He would be thrilled to see this production finally going forward.

Crooked Wood

By Gillian Plowman

Miss Barwick	Doreen Mantle
Andrew Veitch	Nick Waring
Murray Lester	Clive Carter
Sally Veitch	Shona Lindsay
Quentin Gilbey	Alec Walters

Director	Gene David Kirk
Designer	Alice Walkling
Lighting/SoundDesign	Phil Hewitt
Production Manager	Tim McArthur
Stage Manager	Heather Crose
Assistant Director	Helen Broughton
Lighting /Sound Operator	Justin Emrys Smith
Press	Clout Communications (020 7851 8628)
Production Photography	Polly Hancock

Production at Jermyn Street Theatre:
9 September – 4 October 2008

Biographies

CAST

DOREEN MANTLE

Doreen Mantle has given many well known performances for stage and screen, and to date has over 130 credits to her name. Her stage performances include *Voysey Inheritance*, *Tales from Vienna Woods* and the Olivier Award winning *Death of a Salesman* all at the National Theatre. Her West End theatre credits include: *Exchange* (Vaudeville), *84 Charing Cross Road* (Ambassadors), *Mornings at Seven* (Westminster Theatre), *Interpretators* (Queens), *The Seagull* (Duke of Yorks). Further theatre credits include: *Singular People* (King's Head Theatre),*The Birthday Party* (Manchester Contact) for which she was nominated Best Actress in the *Manchester Evening News*; *Hamlet* (Derby Playhouse) which won Best Performance of the Year; *A Night with Mrs Da Tank* and *Going Home* both by William Trevor (King's Head Theatre). Doreen also performed in four other William Trevor plays for television.

Doreen is also well renowned for her many television appearances; credits include: *Jam and Jerusalem* (BBC), *20,000 Streets Under the Sky* (BBC), *Our Friends in the North* (BBC). She is perhaps best known for her role as Mrs Warboys in *One Foot in the Grave* (BBC), which she played for 10 years.

Further to this her film credits include: *In Love and War* (Richard Attenborough), *Mountains of the Moon* (Bob Rafelson), *Yentl* (Barbra Streisand) *The French Lieutenant's Woman* (Karel Reisz), and *Black Jack* (Ken Loach) which won the Cannes Critic Award.

Doreen is delighted to be performing at Jermyn Street Theatre in memory of Dan Crawford and Judy Campbell following her continued relationship with the King's Head Theatre throughout her career.

NICK WARING

Theatre Credits Include: Werewolf/ Clovis in *The Beastly Chronicles of Saki* (Jermyn Street Theatre); Bubbs in *The Unblest* (King's Head); Clive Monkhams in *After October* (Chichester Festival Theatre, Richmond and Greenwich); Johnnie Tanner in *Misalliance* (Theatre Clywd and Birmingham); D'Artagnan in *The Three Musketeers* (UK Tour); Maecenas in *Antony and Cleopatra* (Moving Theatre tour directed by Corin and Vanessa Redgrave); The German Soldier in *Liberation of Skopje* (Riverside Studios); Algernon in *The Importance of Being Earnest* and Roy Selfridge in *Biloxi Blues* (Salisbury Playhouse), Pete in *Democracy* (Bush); The Notary in *The Bells* (Riverside Studios); Romeo in *Romeo and Juliet* (Harrogate); Hastings in *She Stoops to Conquer* (Harrogate); Backbite in *School for Scandal* and Konstantin in *The Seagull* (Theatre Clywd) for which he was nominated for the 'Ian Charleston Award' for Best Performance By An Actor Under 30 In A Classical Role; Simon in *Hay Fever* (Theatre Clywd and West End); Tom Jones in

The History of Tom Jones (Belgrade Coventry); Narrator in *Under Milk Wood* (Shaw); Blake in *The Waiting Game* (The Mill At Sonning); Lord Alfred Douglas in *Gross Indecency* (Plymouth and West End); Tony Orford in *Star Quality* (UK Tour and West End); Dorian Gray in *The Picture of Dorian Gray* (Windsor and UK Tour); Christopher in *Trumbo* (Tricycle Theatre, Directed by Corin Redgrave); Geoffrey in *Deadly Nightcap*, Philip in *My Cousin Rachel*, Nick in *Joking Apart* and Alan Wells in *Sweet Revenge* all at Windsor. Nick played the role of Thomas Mowbray in *Richard II* directed by Steven Berkoff (Ludlow Festival); Charles Stratton in *Separate Tables* and Peter in *Strictly Murder* (both The Mill At Sonning), Victor in *Private Lives* (British Theatre Playhouse) Sgt. Trotter in *The Mousetrap* (St Martin's Theatre) and most recently in a tour of *A Business of Murder*.

Television credits include: Robert Smith in *London's Burning* (LWT), Rupert in *Harry Enfield and Chums* (Tiger Aspect), Salerio in *The Merchant of Venice* (Tetra Films), Dimitri in *Ellington* (Yorkshire Television), *Out of the Past* (Mentorn Barraclough Carey), *Holby City* (BBC), Hugh Manning in *Doctors* (BBC) and most recently Rixton in *The Bill* (Thames).

Film credits include: Gary in *When Saturday Comes* (Pint o'Bitter Productions), William in *The Asylum* (Nunhead Films) and Jo Jo in *Big Pants*.

CLIVE CARTER

West End credits include: Thomas Cromwell in *A Man For All Seasons* with Martin Shaw (Haymarket); Gooper in *Cat on a Hot Tin Roof* with Brendan Fraser and Ned Beatty (Lyric); Khashoggi in *We Will Rock You* (Dominion Theatre); *Almost Like Being in Love* (Royal National Theatre); Lloyd in *The Demon Headmaster* (Royal National Theatre); Edward VIII in *Always* (Victoria Palace); *I Love You You're Perfect Now Change* (Comedy); Prince/Wolf in *Into the Woods* for which Clive was nominated for an Olivier Award (Phoenix); Dr Lyman Sanderson in *Harvey* (Shaftesbury), original company/ Javert in RSC/Cameron Mackintosh's *Les Miserables* (Barbican/Palace). Clive created the role of Raoul in Andrew Lloyd Webber's *Phantom of the Opera* (Sydmonton/Her Majesty's); Kane in *Someone Like You* (Strand); Dean Martin in *The Rat Pack* (Palladium); Ben Marco in *The Manchurian Candidate* (Lyric); Mark Antony *Julius Caesar,* Cassio in *Othello* (Mermaid); Demetrius in *A Midsummer Nights Dream,* Tranio in *The Taming of the Shrew,* O'Flaherty in Shaw's *O'Flaherty VC* and Martin in *Connecticut Yankee* (New Shakespeare Company); Harry Berlin in *Luv,* and *Side By Side By Sondheim* (Jermyn Street Theatre).

Other parts include: Title role in *Henry V*, Malcolm in *Macbeth* (York Theatre Royal) Orlando in *As You Like It* (Northcott Theatre Exeter); Sir Wilful Witwood in *Way of the World,* Soranzo in *'Tis Pity She's a Whore* (Nottingham Playhouse); Joel in *If Winter Comes* (Leicester

Haymarket) Professor Higgins in *My Fair Lady* (Sheffield Crucible)

Film: *The DaVinci Code* playing Police Captain at Biggin Hill, directed by Ron Howard playing opposite Tom Hanks and Sir Ian McKellen. He played the role of Peter Soam in the feature film *Chromophobia*, alongside Ralph Fiennes and Penelope Cruz, directed by Martha Fiennes; Dr Edward Marsh in *Learning to Love the Grey*, Maverick Films for the BBC; Private Shaw in *Officer*; and Robert James in *Death on the Nile*.

Television & Radio includes: Mayhew in *Dalziel & Pascoe* (BBC); Dialulus in *Roman Mysteries* (BBC); Director in *Johnny Shakespeare* (BBC): Mac in *Eastenders* (BBC); Dr Peter Andrews in *Doctors* (BBC); John Ryland in *The Bill* (Thames); Dudley Blake *In Rep* (Granada); Dicky Heart in *Number 73* (Meridian); Barton in *Mitch* (Yorkshire); PC Abraham in *Diamonds* (LWT); and Gary in *Taking Stock* (LWT). Gooper in *Cat on a Hot Tin Roof* (BBC Radio 3)

Directing: *Gala Concert* to celebrate ten years Jermyn Street Theatre at the Criterion; *A Resounding Tinkle* (Jermyn Street Theatre); directed and adapted *A... My Name Is Alice* at the Bridewell Theatre; associate director on *The Rat Pack* (tour and London).

SHONA LINDSAY

Shona is one of the most sought-after ladies in the West End having been the youngest Christine to star in *Phantom of the Opera* at Her Majestys. Other West End roles include: Sandy in *Grease* at The Dominion, *I Love You, You're Perfect Now Change* at The Comedy and Milly Pontipee in *Seven Brides for Seven Brothers* at Theatre Royal, Haymarket, *Same Time Next Year* and *A Chorus of Disapproval* at The Mill at Sonning and most recently has been seen in the role of Rose in the UK Tour of *Aspects of Love*.

Shona made her professional debut in the title role of *Annie* followed by *Secret Diary of Adrian Mole* and *Growing Pains of Adrian Mole* for Thames Television. She left school to join *Crossroads* and played Sara Briggs for two years. To mark the end of the series Shona released the single *Goodbye* for RCA/BMG.

Other theatre roles include: *Cat on a Hot Tin Roof, The Wicked World of Bel Ami, The Provok'd Husband* and *Hobson's Choice* at The New End, *Godspell,* and the national tour of *Singin' in the Rain* opposite Paul Nicholas. In between the national tours of *Seven Brides*, Shona appeared in the thriller *Murdered to Death, Oh What a Lovely War* and *The Mating Game*. Shona was then reunited with Paul Nicholas for the first UK production of the award winning Broadway Musical *Jekyll & Hyde* by Leslie Bricusse.

Shona has appeared in the films *Blush* and *Telephone Detectives* as well as episodes of *Doctors* and *Casualty*. Among her many radio appearances are the musicals *Follies, Call Me Madam, The Dancing Years* and *A Chorus Line* as well as several *Friday Night Is Music Night*.

For further information visit Shona's website: www.shonalindsay.co.uk and www.bgcltd.org

ALEC WALTERS

Recent productions include: King George VI (Bertie) in *The Dorchester* at Jermyn Street Theatre, directed by Lynda Baron; Lord Netherend in *Cry Blue Murder!* (Heartbreak Productions national tour); Benedick in *Much Ado About Nothing* at Jermyn Street Theatre (Actors Company Rep Season); Lane/Gribsby/Chasuble in *The Importance of Being Earnest* (Heartbreak Productions national tour); Reverend Shandy in *The Lying Kind*; Dr Bradman in *Blithe Spirit* for Harpenden Theatre; Peter in *Gobsmack* for Foundling Theatre at The White Bear; Polonius in *Hamlet* for the Cambridge Shakespeare Festival; R Levy QC in *The Prostitutes' Padre* at the Greenwich Playhouse. Commercials include: the lead in the recent *Trident Gum Factory Viral*. TV includes: *Rosemary and Thyme* and *The Bill*, in addition to a number of short films; one of which gained a prize at the Cherbourg Film Festival.

CREATIVE TEAM

GILLIAN PLOWMAN

Gillian won the Verity Bargate award in 1988 with *Me and My Friend*, a poignantly funny play about the release of four patients from a psychiatric hospital into the community. It was first produced at the Soho Poly Theatre in 1990 and at the Chichester Festival Theatre in 1992.

The Purity Game formed part of the opening season of Chichester's Minerva Theatre Studio in 1989. *Storm* was produced in Hastings and London's Soho theatre by Freehand Theatre Company in 2000/01.

Radio plays for the BBC include *The Wooden Pear* in 1991 starring Anna Massey, *Philip and Rowena* in 1993 with Leslie Phillips and Renee Asherson, *A Sea Change* in 1995 with Jenny Funnell and *David's Birthday* in 2000 with Amanda Root and Clare Holman. A film script *Daisyworld* was commissioned by Paramount Pictures. *Boniface and Me* was broadcast in December 2007, featuring Harriet Walter.

In 1996, Gillian's play *Padlocked* formed part of the Etcetera Theatre's One-Person Play Festival and *Imagine Imogen* was read at the London New Play Festival in 1997.

Full-length plays include *Moments of Glory,* which received a rehearsed reading at the Nuffield Theatre in November 1998, *Another Fine Mess* was toured by the PostScript Theatre Company in 1998/99 and *Pits,* which was a runner up in the 2004 King's Cross Award for new writing.

As well as *Me and My Friend*, plays published by Samuel French include *Beata Beatrix, Cecily, Close to Croydon, David's Birthday, The Janna Years, A Kind of Vesuvius, Philip and Rowena, Two Summers, Umjana Land, There's None So Blind, Tippers, Two Fat Men, Touching Tomorrow, The Allotment* and *The Window Cleaner*, published in 2007.

Gillian's full-length play, *Yours Abundantly, from Zimbabwe* directed by Annie Castledine is produced at the Oval House Theatre, London, during Black History Month, October 2008.

GENE DAVID KIRK

Gene David Kirk is the Programming Director for Theatre 503 in London: responsible for finding, nurturing and developing emerging artists for a theatre dedicated to new work in all forms. As well as *Crooked Wood* by Gillian Plowman at the Jermyn Street Theatre 2008, Gene's directing credits include the world premieres of *Amir: The Lost Prince of Persia* (Theatre503), *Elgar & Alice* by Peter Sutton (UK Tour), *Coming Up For Air* by George Orwell, adapted by Dominic Cavendish (Assembly Rooms Edinburgh), *The Ox and The Ass* by Gillian Plowman, *The Ash Boy* by Chris Lee (Theatre503), *Equus, Aladdin, Shakers* (Colchester) *Arabian Nights* (Key, Peterborough), *Silly Cow, Keeping Tom Nice, Cinderella* (Weeze, Germany). As a writer Gene's first play *Where & When* was staged at The Cockpit in 2001. His second play *All Alone* was staged at the Edinburgh Festival in 2005 where it received The Stage: *Best of the Fest* and Attitude: *Pick of the Fringe*. At the International Dublin Gay theatre Festival 2006 Gene was nominated for The Oscar Wilde Award for Outstanding Achievement in Writing for Theatre 2006. *All Alone* was then staged in London, August 2007, before it moved to New York at the Soho Playhouse, off-Broadway. *Snowdrop*, his current play, is being read by London theatres with a view to production, and he is developing a new play on human trafficking called *Slagheap*. Later this year Gene will be directing the world premiere *Claws* by Dominic Mitchell.

ALICE WALKLING

Alice graduated from the Motley Theatre Design Course in 2005, where she studied under Alison Chitty, Ashley Martin Davis and Anthony Lamble. Design credits include *Yorgjin Oxo – The Man* (Theatre 503), *Ash Boy* (Theatre 503). Assistant design credits include *Afterbirth* and *Factory Girls* (Arcola Theatre) and *Jackets* (Theatre 503).

Alice also works as a Costume Design Assistant in Television and Film and designed the costumes for the recent black comedy *City Rats*.

PHIL HEWITT

Trained at Theatr Clwyd (1987–90), and LAMDA (1990–92). He has designed lighting and/or sound for well over 50 productions, from fringe to regional to West End, and abroad.

Lighting credits include the premieres of Dennis Kelly's *Debris*, Duncan Macmillan's *The Most Humane Way to Kill a Lobster*, and Jennifer Farmer's *Breathing*. Sound design credits include: Gary Owens' *Cancer Time*, and Sir Peter Hall's production of *An Absolute Turkey*.

Lighting and Sound credits include: *All Alone* (Edinburgh, Dublin, New York), and *Coming up for Air* by George Orwell, adapted by Dominic Cavendish. Phil was an Associate Director of Theatre 503 in Battersea (2002–2006), a member of the theatre ensemble Brian (for whom he wrote the piece *Manband* in 2005).

Phil DJs irregularly, and composes electronica even more sporadically.

**Jermyn
Street
Theatre**

THE STORY OF
JERMYN STREET THEATRE

Welcome to what was once the changing rooms for the staff of the Getti (formerly Spaghetti House) restaurant upstairs. In late 1991, Howard Jameson had a vision – to transform the space into a luxury studio theatre in the heart of the West End.

In April 1994, after receiving all planning permission, the Trustees started work; materials, expertise and services to the value of £280,000 were donated by 56 British companies and with a major donation from Laings Builders, our challenge was complete. We opened our doors in August 1994.

Our efforts were further rewarded by a National Lottery Grant from The Arts Council of England, enabling us to provide even better facilities for our customers. Our aim is to provide talented new actors, directors and writers with the opportunity to be recognised and given a platform in the best West End studio theatre. In smart, comfortable surroundings and with the aid of other members of the profession, our goal is to raise funds for other worthwhile charity causes during the year through the medium of our entertainment schedule.

The theatre is run by the Trustees, who are all volunteers, and may well be serving you in the bar tonight or might have sold you your ticket. This is the story of Jermyn Street Theatre. We have an unshakeable passion to help those in need. The Trustees of the theatre would like to invite you or your company to become a sponsor. This can either be in sponsoring a chair, programmes, a production or even the theatre itself. This will in turn help us to help others fulfil their dreams.

The Producers wish to thank the following who without their support, love and assistance this first in-house production would not have happened.
Lea Darby, Howard Jameson, Clive Banks, Coutts Charitable Trust, Rex Bunnett, Barry Serjent, Susan Hampshire, Samuel French Ltd, Victor Lownes, Mrs Mary Baum, Mrs J Beveridge, Leonard Ambroski, Robert Gardiner, Tony Tiffany, Mr N Riley, Julian & Emma Kitchener-Fellowes, Paul Dunnett, Marchioness of Londonderry. Not forgetting Gillian Plowman for the play, Gene Kirk for agreeing to direct and of course darling Judy Campbell and Dan Crawford.

Gentlemens' shirts and ties donated by Herbie Frogg, Jermyn Street.
Hat Boxes donated by Bates of Jermyn Street.

Finally all the staff and volunteers at Jermyn Street Theatre, because without them we could not possibly operate.
My deepest gratitude to you all

Penny Horner. Producer for JERMYN STREET THEATRE

CROOKED WOOD

Characters

MISS BARWICK

ANDREW VEITCH

MURRAY LESTER

SALLY VEITCH

QUENTIN GILBEY

For my friends

Act One

Lights up on Crooked Wood.

'Crooked Wood' is a big old Victorian house, unchanged by time. The hall is of panelled wood with a carved wooden staircase offstage. The hall contains a Lalique mirror. There is a door, which leads to the kitchen.

There is also a beautiful japanned chest which is partially covered by clothes. The sitting room is full of treasures. There are books behind glass on shelves, a fine piano, a selection of beautiful pieces of furniture, a chaise longue and a handsome bureau. On shelves and tables are photographs and rich and colourful artefacts of pottery and china.

It is a late Monday afternoon in October. The overhead light in the sitting room has gone off (due to the doorbell ringing).

MISS BARWICK has let VEITCH in.

VEITCH: I've come to apologise.

MISS BARWICK: For the rats?

VEITCH: For the behaviour of Mr Stephens.

MISS BARWICK: What did he do?

VEITCH: Mr Stephens came to visit you earlier on this afternoon. From Golden Future Properties. The Managing Director, Mr Lester, has asked me to come round and apologise.

MISS BARWICK: Oh yes, Mr Stephens. He wasn't interested in the rats either.

VEITCH: No?

MISS BARWICK: But a very nice young man.

VEITCH: Very nice, yes, but sometimes a little short.

MISS BARWICK: Quite as tall as you.

VEITCH: Brusque. You didn't really agree with each other.

MISS BARWICK: I thought he was very agreeable. Except over the rats. Apparently he was born in the Lebanon. His mother was Lebanese. Which would explain his attitude to rats.

VEITCH: Yes.

MISS BARWICK: I knew Beirut when it was a beautiful city. My father took me on a visit. Before all those terrible things happened to it. Wars. How many times in my lifetime have there been wars? Would you like some tea, Mr…er.

VEITCH: Veitch. Andrew Veitch. Tea…er…

MISS BARWICK: I'm quite in the swing of tea today, as they say. Although swing isn't what swing was.

VEITCH: Thank you Mrs Barwick.

MISS BARWICK: Miss. Earl Grey?

VEITCH looks at his watch.

Are you in a hurry?

VEITCH: No. I'd like some Earl Grey. Thank you very much, if it's not too much trouble. Isn't there a light in here?

MISS BARWICK: Yes, there is a light, but it went out when you rang the doorbell. The wiring's mercurial. It might come on if you shut the front door a little harder.

He looks at her.

Would you mind?

He goes back to the front door, opens it and shuts it harder. The overhead light comes on in the sitting room.

Ah, there's my torch. I can never find it in the dark.

VEITCH: It's dangerous, you know.

MISS BARWICK: The torch?

VEITCH: The wiring.

MISS BARWICK: Exactly.

She picks up the torch from a low table and holds it to her. VEITCH returns to the sitting room and stares in wonder at the contents.

VEITCH: Did Mr Stephens discuss money at all?

MISS BARWICK: Oh yes, well the Lebanese do. It's much easier selling houses in the Lebanon, you know. Miss Docherty sold her house and there was so much fuss with solicitors and surveyors and searches and so on. If you want to buy a house in the Lebanon, you just shake hands and hand over the money. He gives you a receipt. What could be simpler?

VEITCH: And that's what Mr Stephens wanted to do.

MISS BARWICK: Well yes, and I said my house wasn't for sale and thanked him kindly for his offer.

VEITCH: Which was?

MISS BARWICK: Seven hundred thousand pounds. I was shocked.

VEITCH: I can understand why.

MISS BARWICK: And then he went up to eight, Mr Veitch.

VEITCH: I know, Miss Barwick. You didn't feel like shaking hands with him?

MISS BARWICK: Eight hundred thousand pounds for somewhere like this? I think he was talking in Lebanese pounds. How long has he been in England, Mr Veitch?

VEITCH: I believe he came as a child.

MISS BARWICK: And then he wanted to give me nine hundred thousand pounds.

VEITCH: That's what he was authorised to do.

MISS BARWICK: Lebanese pounds?

VEITCH: Sterling, Miss Barwick, sterling!

MISS BARWICK: It's not worth nine hundred pounds in its present state. It's leaking, it's creaking, there's damp in the bedrooms and the books, everything stands at more or less than a right angle and there are cracks I can get my fingers into.

VEITCH: It's in a desirable area.

MISS BARWICK: What's desirable about an area that you can't buy a cabbage in?

VEITCH: Are there no shops nearby?

MISS BARWICK: There used to be a greengrocer. There used to be hot water in the bathroom. Something blew up. And do you know, Mr Veitch, there are no public baths any more.

VEITCH: Do you swim?

MISS BARWICK: Baths. Where you can have a bath.

VEITCH: I didn't know that, no.

MISS BARWICK: So I go to the gymnasium.

VEITCH: Do you?

MISS BARWICK: For a shower. I had to join the Over-Fifties Fun Club.

VEITCH waits but there is no more.

VEITCH: So you have no hot water here? Not really very convenient.

MISS BARWICK: It certainly isn't. Would you like to see the staircase? It needs attention.

VEITCH: You haven't thought of moving? Somewhere more convenient?

MISS BARWICK: At my age? Are you any good at staircases, Mr Veitch?

VEITCH: What's wrong with it?

MISS BARWICK: It's rotten in the middle. You have to be very careful and go up the side.

VEITCH: You should be living on one level, Miss Barwick.

MISS BARWICK: How very dull life would be if we all lived it on one level.

VEITCH: No, I mean…

MISS BARWICK: I know what you mean, young man, and you know what I mean. Joys and sorrows. We all have them. Now a ruthless act, then a generous or brave action.

He looks around.

I'm sure you've made many of those.

VEITCH: Ruthless acts?

MISS BARWICK: Brave and generous actions.

VEITCH: No I haven't.

MISS BARWICK: I'm old and wise – I can tell from your face.

VEITCH: I'm sure you can't.

MISS BARWICK: Believe me, I can. You're a good man. I
haven't made the tea yet.

VEITCH: It doesn't matter.

MISS BARWICK: Of course it matters. You'll think me very
vague if I ask you in to tea and forget to get it for you.

VEITCH: Can I help?

MISS BARWICK: Never a ruthless act. Not you.

VEITCH: It's impossible to judge people that quickly.

MISS BARWICK: Look how quickly you were concerned
about my safety with the wiring. Besides, you have to do
it quickly when you're my age or you run out of time. I'm
sure your mother taught you never to ask a lady's age.

Beat.

Eighty-seven.

VEITCH: I know that wisdom comes with age, Miss Barwick…

She smiles at him.

MISS BARWICK: My second young man today. I don't know
what the neighbours would say. If they were still there.

VEITCH: I don't think Stephens could be described as young…

MISS BARWICK: Everyone's young. Now tea…

VEITCH: And it would be very wise of you to let…

The front door bell rings and the light goes off.

MISS BARWICK: Oh dear.

VEITCH: …my company acquire your house…

MISS BARWICK: Would you go Mr Veitch? Little slam…

> *She goes to the kitchen. He goes to the hallway and stops to check his appearance in the mirror. Inpects the mirror itself. Opens the door. LESTER enters. Bangs it shut. The light comes on.*

VEITCH: Murray.

LESTER: I was passing, Andrew. Thought I'd see for myself.

VEITCH: Fucking trust me.

LESTER: My oh my, this is a dump, isn't it. My goodness me.

> *Enter MISS BARWICK..*

MISS BARWICK: My third young man. Earl Grey?

LESTER: Who's he?

VEITCH: This is my boss, Murray Lester.

MISS BARWICK: With a hyphen?

LESTER: No.

MISS BARWICK: Thank you Mr Murray.

LESTER: Lester.

MISS BARWICK: Yes.

LESTER: What for?

MISS BARWICK: Sending me such delightful young men.

> *MISS BARWICK returns to the kitchen.*

LESTER: Is that her?

VEITCH: Yes.

LESTER: What's the problem?

VEITCH: She doesn't want to sell.

LESTER: On Friday morning, Andrew, Vollendorf arrives from the Middle East. He is not a nice man, not a nice man at all, but he's made a lot of money, and if he arrives and finds this site is not available because of one little old lady, he will cut our hands off, Andrew. One hundred and thirty million pounds. Don't fuck up.

VEITCH: I'll work on her.

LESTER: A little accident, Andrew. Slate fell off the roof. Oh how sad.

VEITCH: Risky, Murray, the minute we appear on the scene.

LESTER: Pretend to start fixing up the house.

VEITCH: Me. I don't do fixing.

LESTER: Exactly. You've got the skills of a bull in a china shop. Prove the house is beyond redemption and make her sell.

VEITCH: I'll up the offer. I think she trusts me.

LESTER groans.

All right. If that doesn't work… I'll have a go.

LESTER: So get on with it. If she still refuses to sell, loosen a few more slates in the roof, arrange for some stray vehicle to bump into the gable end and get a dangerous structure notice…

VEITCH: No sweat.

LESTER: How's Sally?

VEITCH: Sally's already started spending my share of the deal. Descended on Sotheby's yesterday armed only with my cheque book. She's gone Japanese. She wants to make it the most beautiful house in London. Salon chinois. Silk curtains. Lacquered furniture – late 18th century stuff.

LESTER: You can afford it, Andrew, as long as you stick with me. How's the renovation going?

VEITCH: Bloody awful. What a mess. And she's throwing a party in the middle of it. Are you coming?

LESTER: All those trendy friends of yours? I don't like Sally's befores. They may appeal to some people. I'll wait till the house is finished and come to her after.

MISS BARWICK enters with a tray and three cups and saucers, milk jug and sugar bowl.

MISS BARWICK: Kettle's just boiling.

Exit MISS BARWICK.

Enter GILBEY.

VEITCH: Good God! Gilbey.

GILBEY: Andrew Veitch. Andy. Well I never.

LESTER: Who's this?

VEITCH: Quentin Gilbey.

LESTER: Who's that?

GILBEY: We used to be partners.

LESTER: What in?

GILBEY: Houses.

VEITCH: Estate agents.

LESTER: Oh yes.

GILBEY: Till Andrew went on to better things. Well, you can see the difference. You've obviously done well for yourself, Andy.

LESTER: You obviously haven't.

VEITCH: Quentin did a law degree. He's a legal beagle.

LESTER: Is he indeed.

GILBEY: Housing and the law.

LESTER: Is that right. What are you doing here?

GILBEY: Refused entry to your office. Refused an appointment by phone.

LESTER: My secretary is very careful who I see.

GILBEY: I bet she is. So I followed you.

He looks round.

Turning somebody else out of a home are you? Developing this site too?

LESTER: Tell your ex to piss off, Andrew.

VEITCH: I don't think you have business here, Quentin.

Enter MISS BARWICK with teapot.

GILBEY: Andy, no. Don't tell me.

LESTER: My old auntie. So get out of her house.

MISS BARWICK beams.

MISS BARWICK: My fourth young man! How do you do?

GILBEY: How do you do?

MISS BARWICK: Will I remember your name?

GILBEY: Quentin Gilbey.

MISS BARWICK: Quentin. Oh. Yes, I'll remember that. I knew a Quentin once.

Well obviously at last, something is going to be done.

Another cup.

She puts the pot down and returns to the kitchen.

GILBEY: What are you planning for this site!

VEITCH: Who are you representing, Quentin, and in what capacity?

GILBEY: A certain borough councillor.

LESTER: What?

GILBEY: Works alongside your man Collins.

LESTER: What man Collins?

GILBEY: On the borough council.

VEITCH: We don't have a man on the borough council.

GILBEY: What about your re-development of the Cardwell site?

VEITCH: We have planning permission for the Cardwell site.

GILBEY: That can be held in abeyance if it is suspected that any omissions in the proper procedure have taken place.

VEITCH: They haven't.

GILBEY: Planning permission cannot be given until it is proved that all owners of property have been notified under section 65 of the Town and Country Panning Act 1990.

VEITCH: Notice was sent to all owners. They had 21 days in which to object.

GILBEY: There are eight owners who are absentee landlords.

VEITCH: We tracked them all down and our man Stephens personally delivered their own notice under Section 65, which took him all the way to Bangladesh in the case of Mr Rahman. He received eight signatures for his trouble.

GILBEY: There were objections.

VEITCH: All overruled.

GILBEY: By your man Collins.

VEITCH: We don't have a man on the council.

GILBEY: Who benefited to the extent of a new car.

LESTER: Now you're making accusations, Gilbey, to a perfectly respectable development company.

GILBEY: My particular councillor is not happy the objections were properly assessed.

VEITCH: We are not in doubt.

LESTER: What's your man's name?

GILBEY: The Walkers, No 3 Elliott Street. The money they get for their house will not be enough to buy them one of a similar standard near to their work.

VEITCH: I personally found them a property of a higher standard.

GILBEY: Higher, yes. Eleventh floor.

LESTER: Slums, Elliott Street.

GILBEY: He now has vertigo and she has clinical depression.

LESTER: We're doing the community a service.

GILBEY: You're razing family homes to the ground.

VEITCH: Legally.

GILBEY: Mr and Mrs Richardson, No 11 Peony Street. Sitting tenants, pre 1988 Housing Act, so they're entitled to stay. He's an invalid.

VEITCH: Court order. Judge decided that Mr Richardson would be better served in a ground-floor council flat with disabled access.

GILBEY: Collins again.

LESTER: He obviously has a heart of gold, whatever you may say about him.

GILBEY: The Richardsons didn't want to move.

LESTER: Some people don't know what's good for them.

GILBEY: Ron and Jeannie Macclesfield. Bought their house when they were married. Have lived in it for nearly fifty years. They don't want to sell it. They don't want it bulldozed down. They want to die in it. They objected. How can planning permission have been granted?

VEITCH: Compulsory purchase.

GILBEY: Never done these days.

VEITCH takes a file out of his briefcase and holds it in front of GILBEY.

VEITCH: Every now and then, it is.

Pause.

The council, you see, want that site developed. They get a set of offices out of it. Surely your man knows that?

GILBEY: Whatever happened to your principles?

VEITCH: Prosperity is the best protector of principles.

GILBEY: Tearing down houses is like tearing flesh with a rusty knife. You get a gaping wound emptying its life blood into the rubble.

LESTER: What!

GILBEY: Festering sores break out in a disrupted community. The neighbourhood spirit disintegrates. Young people turn to drugs and crime. People get killed. Children get abused and grannies get mugged and robbed. People get depressed when you knock their homes down. People commit suicide. Don't you care about the quality of life?

LESTER: Make sure you don't ruin the quality of yours.

GILBEY: Don't threaten me.

LESTER: Get your nasty little do-gooding nose out of my affairs.

He mimes some physical threat (throat cut?).

VEITCH watches silently.

GILBEY: Obviously very practised at turning a blind eye, Andy.

LESTER: Just a warning.

GILBEY: Meet me for a drink for old times' sake?

VEITCH: No thanks.

GILBEY nods and goes.

LESTER: Sort him.

Enter MISS BARWICK with another cup and saucer.

MISS BARWICK: Oh. Has Quentin gone?

LESTER: And sort her!

MISS BARWICK: He will, I'm sure.

LESTER: This house is a dump. Mrs…

MISS BARWICK: Miss.

VEITCH: Barwick.

LESTER: Take the money and run.

MISS BARWICK: To…?

Exit LESTER, taking the last cigarette out of a packet which he throws down. VEITCH picks it up.

VEITCH: I'm sorry about that.

MISS BARWICK: I used to smoke. It was the fashion. I've been through so many fashions. Are you a fashionable young man?

VEITCH: My wife likes me to be.

MISS BARWICK: What's her name?

VEITCH: Sally.

MISS BARWICK: Short for Sarah?

VEITCH: No. Just Sally.

MISS BARWICK: Are you in love with her?

VEITCH: Of course.

MISS BARWICK: The divorce rate is so high these days, one wonders about love. Are you good friends?

VEITCH: Best friends, I would say.

MISS BARWICK: And what about children?

VEITCH: Long way down the list.

MISS BARWICK: There's nothing more important.

VEITCH: We're not ready yet.

She pours the tea.

MISS BARWICK: It's amazing how fashions go round in circles – turn-ups, Oxford bags, wavy hair – all the thing again.

VEITCH: Not exactly Oxford bags, Miss Barwick.

MISS BARWICK: I watched the boat race once, you know.

VEITCH: Oxford Cambridge?

MISS BARWICK: 1937. With a very fashionable young man. We were good friends too. And in love. I was only seventeen but you know when love strikes at seventeen, it stays with you forever.

She looks at him.

VEITCH: Was it Quentin?

MISS BARWICK: How very clever of you! It was.

VEITCH: What happened?

MISS BARWICK: Oxford won by three lengths.

VEITCH: With Quentin?

MISS BARWICK: There was a ball afterwards.

VEITCH: Mmm?

MISS BARWICK: I rather left him in the lurch, I'm afraid. Danced with other young men. Well, a ball is a ball and I loved dancing. But all the time I only had eyes for him. I thought he knew that, but I was wrong. He was jealous and he was hurt.

VEITCH: Did he get over it?

MISS BARWICK: No. No he didn't.

She goes to look in the mirror.

He stopped coming for tea.

We used to look in this mirror together and imagine it was a camera taking pictures of us – we would make funny faces.

Then it was just me and I didn't know that the years would go by without somebody to make faces at in the mirror.

Miss Docherty just wouldn't.

VEITCH: There must have been other suitors?

MISS BARWICK: Not with funny faces.

VEITCH joins her and they gradually make faces at each other.

VEITCH: Is this a Lalique? The mirror?

MISS BARWICK: Yes, one of his early ones.

VEITCH: (Worth a fortune).

MISS BARWICK: He gave it to my father. They actually met, you know. In Baghdad. Poor, poor Baghdad. What are we doing in Iraq, Mr Veitch? It makes me hopping mad, the way people lie to you. The way our prime minister lied to us! Don't you agree? I was on that anti-war march you know.

VEITCH: I didn't see you.

She smiles at him.

MISS BARWICK: The top's rather dirty. Miss Docherty doesn't come any more and I'm afraid I can only reach half way up. Still at least I can check my hat's on straight.

VEITCH: Sally recently bought a Lalique brooche. Art nouveau.

MISS BARWICK: How interesting. I often think he should never have given up making jewellery, but he lost his heart to the endless possibilities of glass. Daddy organised some special sort of sand. This is all my father's stuff. He was in imports and exports, all to do with the building trade. Went all over the world finding new and wonderful materials. My favourite things were Italian tiles. The colours and the patterns you wouldn't believe. We would go to tea in London, to all the big hotels and Daddy would ask to see the bathrooms and declare – my tiles! I found those in Naples!

VEITCH admires a pair of occasional tables.

They're by Morris – of Bristol, not William. Lovely, aren't they?

VEITCH looks at the books.

All my father's books. He was a great reader…all the classics.

VEITCH takes down one of the books, opens it and frowns because it is covered in mould.

Mould. I keep wiping it off.

And the piano is German – Ritmuller – made for Windsor Castle so they say, but cancelled on Albert's death. That's a great pity, I think. She could have consoled herself with music, but she chose to drown herself in grief. One has to look forward, don't you think. Would you like a garibaldi?

Exit MISS BARWICK to the kitchen.

VEITCH tests the stairs with his hands and indeed finds some rotten wood. He turns back into the sitting room and looks at his watch again. He switches on his dictaphone and speaks into it.

VEITCH: Crooked Wood. Stair banisters worth saving and all furniture. Consult Sally Veitch before demolition.

He goes on to list the furniture, tracing with his finger the panelling on a cabinet.

Enter MISS BARWICK behind him.

Inlaid satinwood. Belgian, I think.

VEITCH looks at the bureau.

And possibly a Weisweiler bureau.

MISS BARWICK: You know about furniture?

He switches off the dictaphone.

VEITCH: Sally's an expert. Trained at Sotheby's. I try to learn from her.

MISS BARWICK: Is she any good at staircases?

VEITCH: She has a nose for things neglected and an eye for their potential return to beauty. She knows what needs doing.

MISS BARWICK: I know what needs doing. How does she get it done? Do you do it?

VEITCH: She won't let me touch anything in the house. No, she knows all the right people.

MISS BARWICK: She won't let you do anything?

VEITCH: Doesn't trust me. Do It Yourself, Andrew, she says, is for other people.

MISS BARWICK: But it's your house.

VEITCH: Yes, but I'm not very good. The thing is, I like it, when there's time. Renovating odd bits of furniture. I'm very much on the learning curve – I practise on bits from the junk shop.

MISS BARWICK: I love wood. It lives and breathes and talks to you. I wanted to be a carpenter when I was a girl.

VEITCH: Did you?

MISS BARWICK: But of course, girls were not apprenticed as carpenters. I was determined though to earn my own living, which Mummy and Daddy agreed to – provided, of course, that I lived at home.

VEITCH: So what did you do?

MISS BARWICK: Millinery. Hats for all occasions. Including Ascot. Stupendous hats. I made one once for Queen Elizabeth. When she was a very new queen just before the war. She remarked on the feathers and wore it several times.

Every hat had a hatbox. Now they have to be fold-up, crease-resistant and machine washable.

VEITCH: Like everything else.

MISS BARWICK: Including old ladies.

MISS BARWICK gets out an old hatbox and opens it, removing a lovely old feathered hat.

VEITCH looks at his watch.

This was the first hat I made that was good enough to be sold in Miss Datchett's shop. My mother bought it.

VEITCH: It's beautiful. Put it on.

She stands in front of the mirror and dons the hat. His mobile phone rings. He answers it.

Veitch.

Yes. No, I don't agree. If they don't start moving their arses, I recommend termination of the contract, pull-out, buy-back and re-sale.

MISS BARWICK shows off the hat.

MISS BARWICK: What do you think?

VEITCH: Very pretty.

The phone rings again.

MISS BARWICK: Is there some trouble?

VEITCH: No, just business.

He answers the phone.

Veitch.

Yes. Yes. Yes, I will.

He switches off.

Sorry.

MISS BARWICK: No wires?

VEITCH: It's a mobile phone.

MISS BARWICK: How does it work?

VEITCH: When it rings, you press the green button.

MISS BARWICK: Then you say 'Veitch'.

She mimics him.

VEITCH: I have to say 'Veitch'. It's my name.

MISS BARWICK: 'Veitch'.

She mimics him again and he smiles.

VEITCH: That was Sally reminding me we're going to a dinner party tonight. I have to be on time.

MISS BARWICK: Yes, of course.

VEITCH: Miss Barwick, I'll keep you in suspense no longer. I have been authorised by my company to offer you a cash payment of one million pounds to vacate this property within the next four days.

MISS BARWICK: Another cup of tea?

VEITCH: Yes. No. That is, by midday on Friday. Please think about it. It's a lot of money for a house in this condition.

MISS BARWICK: Daddy used to love dinner parties. Loved to sit at the head of the table, expounding. The role of any woman was to listen attentively, and prompt occasionally. I expect things are different nowadays?

VEITCH: I would personally undertake to ensure the safe transfer of any articles of furniture or other possessions during the period of rehousing. I assure you of that. They would come to no harm.

MISS BARWICK: And where would I go?

VEITCH: To a lovely hotel for a holiday at our expense whilst we find the ideal residence…

MISS BARWICK: Mr Veitch you're a very kind man and I do appreciate your generosity, but I urge you to spend your money on something else.

VEITCH: You can't carry on living under these conditions.

MISS BARWICK: All this house needs is a little attention.

VEITCH: A little attention! Leaking. Creaking. Cracks you can get your fingers into.

MISS BARWICK: I've made a list of all the trouble spots – in my bureau.

She goes to the bureau.

VEITCH: Miss Barwick, I don't think you understand. I'm offering you a million pounds in cash.

MISS BARWICK: Now where was it?

VEITCH: Miss Barwick, please listen. I've never said this to anyone before and I shall never say it to anyone again. Name your price.

MISS BARWICK: Ah, here we are.

VEITCH: Is there any price at all at which you would consider moving from here?

MISS BARWICK: Mr Veitch, I've never moved. I was born here. This house lived before me and I am determined it will live after. It welcomed me into this life and it has been here for everything I've ever felt, everything I've ever learnt and everyone I've ever loved. It will be here for me when I die. It has never deserted me. I can't desert it. Do you see?

VEITCH: It's falling down around you.

MISS BARWICK: Yes, yes.

She is sad.

I should have done better. And I will.

I see the other houses in the street boarded up, Mr Veitch, deserted by those who lived in them. What will happen to them?

He looks at her.

Knocked down? As long as I stay here, no one will knock down Crooked Wood.

VEITCH: There will come a time after you.

MISS BARWICK: And I have no one to leave it to? No family, no, but someone will love it, Mr Veitch. Someone like you, perhaps.

VEITCH: Someone like me…

MISS BARWICK: Crooked Wood will still be standing, Mr Veitch. As long as I stay here. And maybe so will those other houses too. For it seems you need this one before you can do anything.

Beat.

VEITCH: But you can be so much more comfortable.

MISS BARWICK: Not in my heart, Mr Veitch. This house and I are bound together for the rest of my days. I know that's as far as I can go, but it might just be enough…for the threat to pass.

Beat.

VEITCH: You'll change your mind.

She shakes her head and smiles sweetly.

MISS BARWICK: Now, if you want to practise your renovation skills, is there anything you can do about any of these?

She gives him the list.

VEITCH: I'm not giving up, Miss Barwick. I'll be back tomorrow.

MISS BARWICK: Marvellous.

She gets some overalls out of the trunk.

Daddy's overalls. They will fit you, I can see.

SCENE 2

The next morning – Tuesday. It is a bright morning. There is an array of old galvanised buckets and enamel bowls on the floor. Miss Barwick emerges from the kitchen with another tray of tea. She calls up the stairs.

MISS BARWICK: Mr Veitch! I've made you some tea.

She puts the tray down on the table.

Do be careful, won't you. Back against the wall and come down the side.

VEITCH comes down the stairs, bedraggled and smudged. He wears the overalls.

VEITCH: I know.

MISS BARWICK: How did you get on with the leaks?

VEITCH: It's no good, Miss Barwick. No sooner do you mend one part of the roof, then another hole stares you in the face.

MISS BARWICK: But you have mended one bit?

She hands him a cup of tea.

VEITCH: No. It's impossible.

MISS BARWICK: You can do it, Mr Veitch. I know you think you're no good at mending things, but I trust you. Please have a go.

VEITCH: I can't.

MISS BARWICK: You can! Have faith in yourself. Have courage. Just mend one little hole to start with and that will make things better than they were yesterday. By all accounts, you can't make it worse!

VEITCH: It's pointless.

MISS BARWICK: The fact that you called at my door yesterday is the best thing that's happened to me for years.

VEITCH: I must be honest with you.

MISS BARWICK: You wouldn't be anything else, Mr Veitch. Such an open face…

She dabs his nose with a duster.

It must be very dirty in the roof.

VEITCH: It's a mess. There are birds' nests, woodworm, chewed-up newspapers with mice droppings everywhere, broken slates that need replacing.

MISS BARWICK: I have some slates in the garden shed. Daddy kept quite a few spare ones for emergencies. And there's a long ladder for getting up there.

VEITCH: They all need replacing.

MISS BARWICK: Oh surely not.

VEITCH: And I'm not going up a long ladder onto the roof.

Pause.

MISS BARWICK: No, of course not.

Pause.

She indicates the buckets and bowls.

I've brought these in. Perhaps you could just put them up in the roof under the worst leaks?

VEITCH: And who's going to empty them?

Pause.

There isn't anyone.

MISS BARWICK: I know it would be better to get the slates on, wouldn't it? It's just that nobody will come.

VEITCH: It would be better for you to move. My offer still stands. You could buy a splendid place, warm and comfortable, with no maintenance problems whatsoever.

MISS BARWICK: I'm sure I could hire a man to empty the buckets.

VEITCH: One million pounds, Miss Barwick.

MISS BARWICK: Yes I know.

VEITCH: Will you think about it?

She takes his cup and hands him some buckets.

MISS BARWICK: If you take these up.

He bends over to pick up the buckets. Her eyes are on a level with his backside.

I like bottoms, Mr Veitch, don't you?

He stops in his tracks.

As a little girl, when I only came up to my father's waist, I loved walking behind him and watching the movement of his bottom.

Mummy wore too many skirts…you couldn't see.

She follows him with the bowl to the bottom of the stairs.

She steadfastly refused to be a flapper, which disappointed him I think.

My father was one of those quite intolerable people who are good at everything. He would suddenly have days of great energy. Belle, he used to say. He called me Belle – he couldn't stand Prudence. That was one of the things we had in common, profound dislike of my name. He would teach me the charleston and we would dance around the house all day.

She calls up.

How are you doing?

VEITCH returns for the bowl and takes it up.

VEITCH: All right thank you.

MISS BARWICK: I'll pour another cup of tea.

She hums the charleston. He comes down. She talks as she pours.

My mother was very ill, you see, and Daddy promised her that she could choose my name if only she got well again. Mummy believed in prudence in all things but Daddy called me Belle because he believed in beauty. Belle, he would say, I'm going to do all the windows today – mend the broken sash cords, polish the glass and paint the sills. And he did. Another day he'd have a bedroom decorated, move everything out, buy the wallpaper and just get on with it. It's still the same wallpaper. One day he made me dress up in my Sunday best and he went all around the house photographing every room with me in it somewhere. It was a bright day and the sunlight poured through all the windows at different angles, through the lace curtains, making patterns everywhere.

She looks round, remembering. Then goes to the bureau and takes out an old photograph album. She gives it to VEITCH.

That's a day in the life of Crooked Wood in the early twenties. Daddy had survived the war and his business was prospering. We were very happy.

VEITCH: And Belle was indeed a beautiful child.

MISS BARWICK: Four years old.

He turns the pages.

VEITCH: And is this you?

MISS BARWICK: At twenty-one.

VEITCH: You look sad.

MISS BARWICK: Ah well, you see, it was the middle of the war. Our house was full of people with nowhere to go after the Blitz…but the bombs were still dropping and Daddy had that photograph taken in case I died young.

VEITCH: Beautiful…

MISS BARWICK: How was the dinner party?

VEITCH: There were far too many people expounding. Nobody left to listen. But better than being at home. Sally's having the place stripped from top to bottom and restored to its former glory, with modern facilities. Dust everywhere.

MISS BARWICK: What a very good idea…

She looks at him and round the room.

VEITCH: A very expensive idea.

MISS BARWICK: Do you earn a lot of money, Mr Veitch with…who is it you work for?

VEITCH: Golden Future Properties. Quite a lot, yes.

MISS BARWICK: I'm pleased for you. Dealing with properties must be very hard work. I expect you have some difficult customers to deal with?

VEITCH: Yes. At times.

MISS BARWICK: Where do you live?

VEITCH: Islington.

MISS BARWICK: Miss Docherty used to live in Islington. I took her some flowers once when she had the measles. She was fifty-two at the time and suffered terribly from the spots. Tiny little front room in Islington, it was, you could hardly walk round the bed. But she wanted a view while she was ill so they brought the bed downstairs. Now she's in a nursing home. Completely lost her independence. I do hope she has a decent window.

VEITCH: There are some extremely nice sheltered homes you know where you can remain independent and have a good view, but also the security of a warden on call.

MISS BARWICK: It's too late, Mr Veitch. She's somewhere in the country. Too far for me to visit.

VEITCH: I meant for you.

MISS BARWICK: How kind you are.

VEITCH: No. I'm not. You said you'd think again about selling.

MISS BARWICK: Did I?

VEITCH: If I took the buckets up.

MISS BARWICK: How big is your front room, Mr Veitch?

VEITCH: Miss Barwick, have you thought about it?

MISS BARWICK: I've told you what I thought about it.

VEITCH: Think again.

MISS BARWICK: Are you going to knock it down?

VEITCH: It's going to fall down.

Beat.

MISS BARWICK: Tell me about your house.

VEITCH: We've had a wall removed to make a bigger room. Sally wants it to be the most beautiful house in London.

MISS BARWICK: Then she knows how important houses are. I'd like to meet her.

The mobile phone rings from the pocket of VEITCH's jacket that is hanging on a chair. He answers it.

VEITCH: Veitch.

She smiles at the way he says it and mouths it to herself.

Murray…what? Hang on a minute. Yes I'm at Crooked Wood with Miss Barwick.

MISS BARWICK: Is that that nice Mr Murray?

VEITCH: It is.

MISS BARWICK: Say good morning for me.

VEITCH: Miss Barwick says good morning.

VEITCH's face grimaces at LESTER's reply.

MISS BARWICK: Is he well?

VEITCH: I don't know.

MISS BARWICK: Ask him.

VEITCH: Are you well, Murray?

He grimaces again.

MISS BARWICK waits to hear.

As well as can be expected is what I think he means.

MISS BARWICK: Oh good.

VEITCH: I'll call you, Murray, with progress report. Yes, today!

He puts the phone back in his pocket.

MISS BARWICK: You should have told him you'd mended a bit of the roof. That's progress.

VEITCH: I don't think it's the sort of progress he wants to hear about.

MISS BARWICK: Do you think you might be able to fix the hot water? It would be so marvellous to have a bath before getting dressed. Although they're very kind at the gym, I'm beginning to feel rather guilty that I haven't signed up for an aerobics class or badminton.

VEITCH: I wouldn't worry.

MISS BARWICK: I'm sure it's just some screw that's come loose.

VEITCH: What is?

MISS BARWICK: The hot water boiler.

VEITCH picks up the buckets and bowls resignedly.

VEITCH: I'll put these in the roof first.

MISS BARWICK: Thank you, Mr Veitch.

VEITCH disappears carefully up the stairs and MISS BARWICK takes the tray out to the kitchen. There is a knock at the door. She returns and opens the front door. SALLY VEITCH stands there.

SALLY: Hallo. I'm Sally Veitch. Miss Barwick?

MISS BARWICK: Do come in.

SALLY: Is Andrew here?

She notices the japanned chest with great interest.

MISS BARWICK: He's putting the buckets underneath the leaks. Would you like to sit down? He won't be long.

SALLY looks around. Does not sit.

SALLY: You have quite a collection, Miss Barwick.

MISS BARWICK: They've always been here. I was born into them.

SALLY: Lucky you. Andrew and I – we're making our own collection.

MISS BARWICK: I'm sure it's very beautiful. Like you.

SALLY: At least we'll have exactly what we like.

MISS BARWICK: I like all of this.

SALLY: It's suffering a bit.

Beat.

MISS BARWICK: Can I get you some tea?

SALLY: No, no tea, thank you. Andrew and I hate the stuff.

MISS BARWICK: Oh.

SALLY: Coffee?

MISS BARWICK: I'm afraid I don't have any. Campari?

SALLY: Campari?

MISS BARWICK: It's all I allow myself these days.

SALLY: Campari. Thank you.

SALLY looks around. MISS BARWICK gets a bottle of campari and three crystal glasses from a cabinet. She pours. SALLY has got to the books.

Oh dear.

MISS BARWICK: What?

SALLY: The state of these books.

MISS BARWICK: They're damp, I know.

SALLY: You know? And you've done nothing about it? You really ought to be ashamed of yourself.

MISS BARWICK: I do have a fire in here in the evenings.

SALLY: They are valuable books. Precious books.

MISS BARWICK: My father's. He left them to me.

SALLY: Then you are responsible for these books. They live in your house.

MISS BARWICK: Yes.

SALLY: And look at them! Cockled and warped, stained with mildew. They've even got silverfish.

MISS BARWICK: Have they? Oh dear.

SALLY: They should be kept clean and dry with a constant temperature and relative humidity. Not too much light.

MISS BARWICK: There's not too much light most of the time in here.

SALLY: If you're going to lock them in cabinets, you must make sure there is adequate ventilation. Drill holes in the back. The air must circulate. A saucer of Paradichlorobenzene crystals in the cabinet would discourage mould and insects.

MISS BARWICK downs her campari and pours herself another.

MISS BARWICK: I'm so sorry.

VEITCH comes down the stairs.

I haven't looked after things very well, Mr Veitch.

SALLY and VEITCH exchange glances.

VEITCH: A house this size and a lady your age, especially with Miss Docherty gone, you can't expect to keep everything perfectly.

SALLY: Some things are a lot less than perfect, Andrew. Some things are deteriorating rapidly. Look at this, damp under the veneer. The mirror spotted – my god, it's a Lalique. How could you? The piano...

She plays some notes, half of which don't work.

MISS BARWICK: There are some tunes you can play that don't need all the notes.

SALLY: The piano is on the point of death.

She shuts the piano lid and turns.

Everything is on the point of death, Miss Barwick.

VEITCH: But they are only things. I know it upsets you, Sally, because your training compels you to treasure such works of art. But they are Miss Barwick's things and it doesn't upset her and that's all that matters.

MISS BARWICK: Perhaps I too am on the point of death.

VEITCH: Now that's nonsense. You've a whole new life ahead of you. We'll have everything restored and you can take it with you to a lovely new home.

MISS BARWICK: Excuse me a moment, would you? I just want to...do something in the kitchen. Wash up, yes. Do help yourself to a glass of Campari, Mr Veitch, if you would like to.

She goes to the kitchen.

SALLY: What's the matter?

VEITCH: Her face. She does care about her things.

SALLY: I'm sure she does. But she's not able to.

VEITCH: No.

SALLY: Needs must, Andrew. That was the plan.

VEITCH: It's just...the way she looked at me when I told her she didn't care. As if I'd betrayed her.

SALLY: Cruel to be kind. Her things are deteriorating. They should be saved.

VEITCH: I feel such a shit.

SALLY: Me too.

VEITCH: What?

SALLY: She reminds me of my grandmother. So unable to be able.

VEITCH: Your grandmother's in the right place.

SALLY: I suppose...she taught me that you can love and look after beautiful things, yet still use them. Now she can't... My parents look after her beautiful things...they don't look after her.

VEITCH: You do. You go to see her.

SALLY: She says a hug is more precious than a houseful of antiques.

She pulls herself together.

The staff are brilliant if you pick the right place. Come on, Andrew. Let's get on with Miss Barwick. Murray's got a champagne supper laid on to celebrate this deal.

VEITCH: He lays those on at the drop of a hat.

SALLY: And your cut, darling, is going to finance our master plan. You look very sweet in that outfit.

VEITCH: Little old ladies aren't my scene. I prefer contracts. This is Stephens' playground.

SALLY: Well, he got sent home early for getting his sums wrong. And you got sent in. Andrew Veitch. Lester's best man.

She kisses him.

This really isn't the right place for an old lady to live, is it? Hmmm? She'd be better off nice and warm and cosy somewhere. You didn't tell me about this, by the way.

VEITCH: What?

SALLY goes to the chest.

SALLY: Look at it. It's dirty but it's genuine chinoiserie. See. The nails are wooden. A black japanned chest. English, late eighteenth century, Andrew, which is exactly right.

VEITCH: What for?

SALLY: Andrew! Our house! I also happen to know that the Cantwell oriental stock will be up for auction next month. With this as a centrepiece, it could be fantastic. A first!

VEITCH looks at the chest.

VEITCH: How much is it worth?

SALLY: It'll need a good home, won't it? She probably has no idea of its value. Work on her.

VEITCH: I'm supposed to be working on the bathroom. There's no hot water.

SALLY: Does it matter?

VEITCH: Well yes, she can't have a bath. She has to shower at the gym.

SALLY: The gym!

VEITCH: Works out every morning.

SALLY: No!

VEITCH: No. She's joined the over fifties fun club which means she can have a shower there, though she can't quite manage the fun.

SALLY: My gym wouldn't allow anyone in just to have a shower.

MISS BARWICK comes back in.

MISS BARWICK: About the books. Is it too late for them?

SALLY: Too late?

MISS BARWICK: If I did what you said, would they be all right?

SALLY: They all need cleaning and restoring by a book conservator, Miss Barwick.

MISS BARWICK: And do you know one?

SALLY: Oh yes.

MISS BARWICK: And would it cost a lot of money?

SALLY: I'm afraid so.

Pause.

MISS BARWICK: Would you care to have them? I know that you would keep them in their proper condition.

VEITCH: Miss Barwick, if you were to accept the money that I'm offering you for the house, you could buy yourself a smaller place that would have the right temperature for the books. And all the other things. No damp. And there would be enough money left over to pay to have them restored. You could keep them forever.

MISS BARWICK: Please take them when I go for my shower tomorrow. Take them then. I'll just keep the bible. It was given to father's mother when she was christened, so you can tell how old it is. She was christened Melina Elizabeth. Isn't that a lovely name. You see…

She opens the bible and shows them.

SALLY: When you remove a book from a shelf, you shouldn't grab the top or the sides of the spine, or it will eventually break. You must gently push the books on either side of the one you want further back into the shelf, and you'll get a better grip on the sides of your book. Shelves should never be packed tightly, you see. And if you're getting out a heavy book, you must support the weight of it underneath with your other hand.

MISS BARWICK listens intently.

MISS BARWICK: I know they're going to be happy with you.

SALLY: All right.

VEITCH: No! They're your father's books. You mustn't give them away.

Pause.

SALLY: I'll take them to the conservator anyway. One way or the other, someone is going to have the money to pay for them. I'm going to see the architect now Andrew. And I'm having our things moved into the Grand. It's impossible living in that mess. They've got a small suite available for a couple of months. Penrose suite. Luxury bathroom with Jacuzzi, which is where I'll be between six and seven this evening. Join me, darling. I'll leave your key in reception. We've dinner at Poppy's tonight.

VEITCH: Where the hell were we last night?

SALLY: Pansy's. Goodbye, Miss Barwick and good luck with your move.

MISS BARWICK: I'll see you out.

MISS BARWICK goes to open the front door. SALLY follows her, passes the chest and mouths to VEITCH.

SALLY: I want that.

Exit SALLY through front door. MISS BARWICK comes back into the sitting room and goes to the bookcase. She takes a book down carefully from the shelf as instructed by SALLY and opens it carefully. She is still for a long time as a tear runs down her cheek.

VEITCH sees her tears.

MISS BARWICK: What a lovely, kind, practical person your wife is, Mr Veitch. I can quite see why you're best friends.

VEITCH returns upstairs. She goes to the piano and lifts the lid. She plays a tune, which ignores the keys that do not work. The piano is out of tune.

She winds up her gramaphone and puts on a record – Who Stole My Heart Away. *She takes a yellow duster from her pocket and dusts some of the photos and pictures. The mobile phone rings. She calls up the stairs.*

Mr Veitch!

The phone continues to ring. She picks it up and presses the green button. She mimics VEITCH.

'Veitch.'

She listens to what is obviously a short speech from the other end.

VEITCH comes down the stairs. For the first time, we see him smile with pleasure.

VEITCH: Guess what, Miss Barwick? I've done it!

MISS BARWICK: What?

VEITCH: Had a little go at your bathroom water heater, and hey presto, it works.

MISS BARWICK: Hot water?

VEITCH: Indeed.

MISS BARWICK: Oh how lovely! How clever you are!

VEITCH: If I were you, Miss Barwick, I'd get that enamel bath polished. You can get rid of the stains – Sally's got a solution for that – and the chips can be filled in. It's a beautiful thing.

MISS BARWICK: Original.

VEITCH: And those brass taps, you can't get those for love or money nowadays.

MISS BARWICK: I'll polish them this afternoon. Oh thank you, Mr Veitch. I'm sure we could get this whole place sorted out in no time at all.

VEITCH pulls himself up short.

VEITCH: Ah. Miss Barwick, we must sit down and talk.

MISS BARWICK: Perhaps you could look at the wiring?

VEITCH: Electricity's my weak point.

MISS BARWICK: Daddy had a very useful book – Electrical Wiring in the Home.

She finds the book and gives it to him.

VEITCH: 1925.

MISS BARWICK: That's when he modernised everything.

I answered your moving phone, Mr Veitch. It called whilst you were upstairs. I took a message. I'm sure it was from Mr Murray. I recognised his voice.

VEITCH: Lester. What did he say?

MISS BARWICK: Don't take all fucking day.

VEITCH: Thank you, Miss Barwick.

Act Two

SCENE 1

It is early Wednesday morning. The curtains are drawn shut. MISS BARWICK is in her dressing gown. She has just let VEITCH in. She pulls the curtains back and puts her hand on the light switch.

MISS BARWICK: Good heavens, what an early bird you are, Mr Veitch.

VEITCH: I called round to see you last night. Miss Barwick but I couldn't make you hear.

MISS BARWICK: I never answer the door to anybody after dark. That would be very foolish, don't you think? Door please.

VEITCH: You really should have a telephone.

MISS BARWICK: Now whom would I ring?

VEITCH bangs the door shut and the sitting room light comes on.

Why did you call?

VEITCH: To make sure you were all right.

MISS BARWICK: Just like a son would.

VEITCH: No, because…the house is in a dangerous state, you know.

MISS BARWICK: Sometimes, when I play the piano, I hear orchestras playing. Fills the room. I'm sorry I didn't hear you. Weren't you supposed to be having dinner somewhere?

VEITCH: Had a lot of business to catch up on.

MISS BARWICK: Am I taking up too much of your time?

VEITCH: Of course not.

MISS BARWICK: I am going upstairs to have my bath now. Please help yourself to coffee.

VEITCH: Coffee?

MISS BARWICK: I bought some yesterday. I'm sure you must be getting jolly fed up with Earl Grey.

VEITCH: Thank you, Miss Barwick.

A car stops outside. The sitting room light goes off. Enter LESTER.

MISS BARWICK: May I say how pleased I am with Mr Veitch, Mr Murray. He's done so much for me.

LESTER: Has he?

MISS BARWICK: The leaks, the hot water. Are you any good at electricity?

She shows LESTER that the sitting room light doesn't work.

Mr Veitch, would you mind?

VEITCH: Excuse me, Murray.

He bangs the front door shut and the light comes on.

MISS BARWICK: Thank you dear. You see, Mr Murray, the wiring's in a worse state than a free state, as my father would say.

LESTER: Mr Lester. My first name's Murray.

MISS BARWICK: Would you like to look at it?

LESTER: What?

MISS BARWICK: The wiring.

LESTER: I'm on my way to a very important meeting.

MISS BARWICK: It was nice of you to call and see how we're getting on. So encouraging. Thank you very much.

She goes upstairs.

VEITCH: All she wants is to live in this house until her death.

LESTER: Sounds like a good idea.

VEITCH: What?

LESTER: Her death. Get rid of her and we can collect Vollendorf's millions. He goes somewhere else Friday night if we don't produce.

VEITCH: What if I can't do it?

LESTER: I didn't hear you say that.

His mobile rings.

Mr Vollendorf. How goes it with you? Yeah. Yeah. Me too. Keynes Road. All wrapped up. No problem. Friday. Yeah. Big one. My pleasure, Mr Vollendorf.

He presses for another number.

Amazing, Andrew. You can stand in the scruffy front room of a scruffy house in the back end of London and talk to the other side of the world through a little tiny instrument hardly bigger than your ear.

(*Into the phone.*) Julie? Looks like I've got all afternoon! Me too!

He switches off.

VEITCH: Julie?

LESTER: My wife doesn't understand me.

VEITCH: You've got to work at marriage.

Enter SALLY.

SALLY / VEITCH: (*Together.*) Where the hell were you last night?

LESTER: So I see.

He goes.

VEITCH takes his jacket off and puts the overalls on.

SALLY: I end up at Poppy's on my own. Not a bloody word from you.

VEITCH: I couldn't remember where we were going. I rang. You didn't answer. Did you check your messages?

SALLY: I kept expecting you to turn up.

VEITCH: I haven't a clue where Poppy lives.

SALLY: Yes you do. We were there last week.

VEITCH: Oh that Poppy!

SALLY: Christ, Andrew, get a grip.

VEITCH: I thought we would go together.

SALLY: And both be late? You're spending so much bloody time here.

VEITCH: Why didn't you come home last night?

SALLY: It's a hotel.

VEITCH: You moved into it.

SALLY: Because you kept complaining about the mess at home.

VEITCH: I bet Clive was there?

SALLY: Clive who?

VEITCH: Clive who wants to get into your knickers Clive.

SALLY: Clive's a marble expert.

VEITCH: He obviously wants to get his hands on something warmer.

SALLY: Advising on the Adams fireplace.

VEITCH: Did he stay the night too?

SALLY: I don't know.

VEITCH: Of course you know.

SALLY: I wasn't well, Andrew and I couldn't drive back and you couldn't be bothered to come and fetch me.

VEITCH: I would have done if I'd known where you were.

SALLY: Poppy's!

VEITCH: You shouldn't drink so much.

SALLY: I didn't. It was the food or something. Andrew, I never see you.

VEITCH: Because I'm working my butt off to finance your every whim.

SALLY: Our dream.

VEITCH: So where did Clive sleep?

SALLY: I'm surprised you've got any friends, Andrew, the way you trust nobody.

VEITCH: Where?

SALLY: Not with me!

Pause.

Did you talk to her about the chest?

VEITCH: No.

SALLY: Andrew!

VEITCH: I haven't had time.

SALLY: You never have time to do anything for me!

VEITCH: For Christ's sake, Sally!

SALLY: I'm spending my morning packing up these bloody books! For you!

She is putting the books into a box. There is a loud explosion from upstairs.

VEITCH: Miss Barwick!

SALLY: Oh no!

VEITCH rushes to the stairs. She follows.

VEITCH: Don't come up the stairs!

His mobile phone rings. SALLY answers it.

SALLY: Not now, Murray, there's been an explosion. Miss Barwick may be hurt. What do you mean good!

She is shocked.

Call back!!

VEITCH brings MISS BARWICK down and puts her in a chair. SALLY finds a cardigan/something and wraps it around her. MISS BARWICK has some lacerations on her face.

We must get her to hospital.

MISS BARWICK: It's just the shock from the blast. I'm not injured, honestly. No bones broken.

VEITCH: You are injured.

MISS BARWICK: No really…

VEITCH: Why don't you let me take you to the hospital for a check up?

MISS BARWICK: You've got too much to do here.

SALLY: I'll take you.

MISS BARWICK: They might keep me there.

VEITCH: Overnight possibly, just to make sure you're all right.

MISS BARWICK: And then I wouldn't be here. And who knows what might happen if I'm not here.

Beat.

VEITCH: Then the doctor must come and see you.

MISS BARWICK: If it will make you feel better.

SALLY: I know what will make you feel better.

MISS BARWICK: What?

SALLY: Campari?

MISS BARWICK: Campari.

SALLY: Campari. Andrew.

He gets the drinks.

VEITCH: I'm really sorry.

SALLY gently wipes MISS BARWICK's face with a damp tissue.

MISS BARWICK: It's not your fault.

VEITCH: Of course it is. The boiler, my incompetence.

MISS BARWICK: We had hot water!

VEITCH: You could have been killed due to my stupidity.

MISS BARWICK: It's a very old boiler.

SALLY: Not too bad. (*The face.*)

MISS BARWICK: You can take the books to hospital.

SALLY hesitates.

Take them. Please. Make *them* better.

SALLY takes the box out.

You've done nothing but try to help me, Mr Veitch.

VEITCH: I've done nothing but hurt you.

MISS BARWICK: No you haven't. I know how much you care. That guides you. I'd like to have had a son like you. Your mother must be very proud of you.

VEITCH: No...she's...

Beat.

MISS BARWICK: Oh I'm sorry. You've lost her.

VEITCH: She lost me.

She waits. Nothing.

MISS BARWICK: One advantage of being old is that you can be nosy...

VEITCH: I didn't know my mother.

MISS BARWICK: How sad.

VEITCH: You know...you read about it. Abandoned baby. I never found out who she was. Or my father of course... long time ago...

Andrew Veitch. Just made up. Who's he?

MISS BARWICK: Someone to be proud of.

VEITCH: There's no one to be proud of me.

MISS BARWICK: Oh yes there is.

She holds out her hand.

What happened then?

VEITCH: I was a Barnardo's boy.

MISS BARWICK: Perhaps you have great strength because of it.

VEITCH: They looked after us well. I was determined to be rich. Have a home that others would envy. When I met Sally, I didn't believe that anyone like her would look at me; that I could give her everything her parents could... everything she wanted.

MISS BARWICK: Well you have.

VEITCH: I've shown them.

MISS BARWICK: Daddy met Dr Barnardo you know.

VEITCH: Your father seems to have met everyone…

MISS BARWICK: That was the point of Daddy! He would love to have met you. He would have been proud of you.

VEITCH: No…

MISS BARWICK: Because you are not only successful, but compassionate. That was Daddy's ideal. He sent money to Dr Barnardo's all his life because he wanted to help those orphans grow up to be hard-working, successful young men who found a way to help others.

VEITCH: I don't help anyone but myself.

MISS BARWICK: Of course you do. You're helping me. The true route to happiness, he always said. Personally, and it's just between you and me, I have often found that helping some people can be very tiresome. I hope I'm not one of them…?

VEITCH: Of course you're not.

She holds out her hand and he takes it.

MISS BARWICK: Daddy left a lot of money to Barnardo's in his will, although I sometimes wonder whether he should have put a little more aside to look after the house.

Pause.

VEITCH: I'll look after the house, Miss Barwick.

MISS BARWICK: Oh will you?

VEITCH: I will. I promise.

MISS BARWICK: I believe you.

VEITCH: I'll just go up and check on that boiler – don't want another explosion.

He goes up stairs. She gets up and pours herself another campari. The doorbell rings. She goes and comes back into the room with an envelope which she opens. She stares at the letter. VEITCH comes back.

It's OK. Miss Barwick? What's that?

MISS BARWICK: It's a legal document. I signed for it.

VEITCH: Oh no!

MISS BARWICK: A Dangerous Structure Notice.

She holds it out. He reads.

VEITCH: *The Borough of Northam requires you to vacate the premises within 24 hours. If you will gather your immediate belongings, you will be collected at 4 pm tomorrow, Thursday 25 October and transferred to alternative accommodation provided by the council. I apologise for any inconvenience, but as you will appreciate, we are acting in the interests of your own safety. A Dangerous Structure Notice has been placed on your house.*

MISS BARWICK: Rubbish. It's not dangerous, it's not. It's been safe all these years.

VEITCH: Of course it has.

MISS BARWICK: I'm not going.

VEITCH: No.

He steadies her.

MISS BARWICK: It says they've done an inspection.

He nods.

When did they do that? I never saw anybody.

VEITCH: It's only a temporary order. We'll do another inspection, prove that it's not dangerous and get the order rescinded.

MISS BARWICK: Is that possible?

VEITCH: I'll phone Quentin.

MISS BARWICK: He became engaged to somebody else.

VEITCH: Quentin?

MISS BARWICK: Yes. He jilted me. I didn't dance with all those young men, you know. Pride. So silly. It was him, dancing with all those bright young things. He was a fashionable

young man and he needed to marry someone with more
position than I had.

VEITCH: He was a very foolish young man.

MISS BARWICK: But he died in the war so I would have lost
him anyway. Don't let me down, Mr Veitch.

He kisses her on the cheek.

SCENE 2

Thursday morning. GILBEY and VEITCH are drinking coffee.

GILBEY: So Andy, what happened on the road to Damascus?

VEITCH: Give me your professional opinion of this house.

GILBEY: I've seen worse.

VEITCH: It's the last house on the Keynes Road site.

GILBEY: You're the developers?

VEITCH: With Willy Vollendorf.

GILBEY: Wants to impose more architectural monstrosities on
the skyline of London?

VEITCH: Titanium office blocks with en suite clinics for the
mega rich. All up in time for the world's spotlight on 2012.

GILBEY: Now you're getting my dander up. Real estate is
going to be at a premium anyway because businesses and
landlords want to buy up places then sell or hire at inflated
prices.

VEITCH: Vollendorf doesn't like being crossed, Quentin, and
neither does Lester.

GILBEY: I gathered that.

VEITCH: They're dangerous.

GILBEY: You're risking more than I am. Why?

VEITCH: Miss Barwick doesn't want to move.

GILBEY: Tried turning the electricity off. Prising off roof slates.
Loosening the banisters?

VEITCH: I know you'll find this hard to believe, Quentin but those are exactly the things I've been trying to put right. I want to save the house.

GILBEY: My God.

VEITCH: She's had a dangerous structure notice. She's got until four this afternoon to get out.

He gives the notice to GILBEY who reads it.

GILBEY: Temporarily.

VEITCH: Oh, come on. Once she's out, something might just have given way before she returns. Profuse apologies, then everyone gets used to it. And if she won't go, something will give way with her under it and everyone's backsides are covered because she's had this.

GILBEY: Backhander was it?

VEITCH: Man on the council.

GILBEY: How much is the site worth?

VEITCH: Hundred and thirty million.

GILBEY: We're going to need our bullet proof vests, aren't we?

VEITCH: Thanks, Quentin.

GILBEY: I had a look round on the way in. The flank wall's bulging and the chimney stack's unsafe. But the wall's already been shored up and they can't touch her on that. All we have to do is remove the chimneystack and get the right inspector along.

VEITCH: That's all?

GILBEY: This place isn't in bad shape, despite the efforts of bastards like you.

VEITCH: Right.

GILBEY: I spend my life fighting for the rights of people living in worse places than this.

Meaningful beat.

Houses on the Cardwell site.

VEITCH: I'll try.

GILBEY: More than that.

VEITCH nods.

VEITCH: How do you make ends meet?

GILBEY: I don't. Come on, jacket off.

VEITCH: What?

GILBEY: Get up the ladder and knock the chimneystack down.

VEITCH: Just like that?

GILBEY: Just like that. I've got some tools in the car – I'll leave them by the door. Make sure it doesn't fall on anyone… I'm going to get cement and a couple of brickies I can trust.

Enter MISS BARWICK from the kitchen.

MISS BARWICK: I've put a shepherd's pie in the oven.

VEITCH: Miss Barwick, we're going to knock your chimney down.

GILBEY: It's the bit that's unsafe.

MISS BARWICK: Where will the smoke go?

GILBEY: We have to do it to get the notice rescinded. We can build a new one later.

MISS BARWICK: How very kind. Do you like shepherd's pie?

GILBEY: Yes!

VEITCH: Yes!

GILBEY: I must go. To work, Andy.

Exit GILBEY. VEITCH starts putting on his overalls.

MISS BARWICK: Do you know, I would be so pleased if you'd call me Belle.

VEITCH: Andrew. Don't go outside will you, Belle. I'm off to knock the chimneystack down.

She goes into the kitchen. Enter LESTER, carrying a demolition mallet.

LESTER: What's this? Murder weapon.

VEITCH: Dunno. Workmen must have left it.

LESTER: What was that smart arse Gilbey doing here?

VEITCH: Apparently she's quite within her rights to challenge the notice.

LESTER: If she's not out nice and quiet by four o'clock this afternoon, something will have to fall on her head.

VEITCH: So you said.

MISS BARWICK comes out of the kitchen.

MISS BARWICK: Oh Mr Murray, how nice to see you. Perhaps you could hold the ladder for Mr Veitch. I'm so worried about him.

LESTER: I can't do that. I've got a bad back.

MISS BARWICK: I haven't.

She goes very carefully upstairs.

LESTER: I've a very strong suspicion you've been fucking me about Andrew. What is it? Eh?

VEITCH: All right. This house has been home to the same person for eighty-seven years. It's leaking, it's damp. It's grubby. It's peeling but it's survived. It's survived. There's no good reason why it should be destroyed. You've got enough space without this one.

LESTER: This one is right in the middle!

VEITCH: It would be a challenge.

LESTER: Vollendorf would not be interested.

VEITCH: Find someone else?

LESTER: I don't believe I'm hearing this. How did you get rich then? How did you afford your tasteful Victorian house on four floors, filled with antiques and a prestige car each for you and the missus parked outside? You didn't get that from helping old ladies cross the road. You got that from the Barnwell Street development. Remember that? Council with a waiting list of four thousand? You got the properties from under their noses and it's now a highly profitable executive terrace. Hopgood Street…how the hell you got rid of those tenants I'll never know, but the rent we take from those offices is why you're my Number 2. Carmody Street, the Elephant, Camberwell Tower…a record to be proud of. All right, you had to be a bastard now and then, but you and I know that's the only way to get this fucking country moving.

Pause.

You and I also know, Andrew, that a bit of information let slip in the wrong direction and my Number 2 could be facing charges of very dodgy dealing.

VEITCH: Acting on your orders.

LESTER: I'm as clean as a whistle.

VEITCH: Like hell you are.

LESTER: I've made sure of it. Andrew, Andrew, we're good mates, good partners. Don't let a little tin pot house come between us.

VEITCH: Give me one more day.

LESTER: One more day and Vollendorf's here. She goes this afternoon. After that, you make sure some large lorry gets stuck in reverse and bumps into Crooked Wood. Ah shame. Still it was unsafe. A nominal amount of compensation is in order – Golden Future Properties will pay that. It amazes me, Andrew, that I have to be telling you your job. And if Sally wants the staircase and the furniture, she'd better get her finger out. By the way, you're booked on a flight to Amsterdam this evening. Vollendorf has a bank account there and I want it checked out before we sign tomorrow. You'll be back in time for the celebrations. My back's been playing me up something awful lately, Andrew, I ought to see Julie more often… leave things in your hands a bit more… I don't want any mistakes, Andrew. None.

He swings the mallet round and lets it drop on the floor.

Could do a lot of damage that.

He turns to go as SALLY enters, wearing an attractive hat.

Sort him out!

Exit LESTER.

SALLY: Andrew...?

VEITCH: I've got a chimneystack to knock down.

SALLY: What?

VEITCH: She's had a dangerous structure notice and that's the bit that's dangerous.

SALLY: ...?

VEITCH: She has to get out by four this afternoon unless we make it safe. Quentin's helping me.

SALLY: But we want her out, don't we? Andrew? What are you doing?

VEITCH: Getting the Notice rescinded.

SALLY: Why?

VEITCH: She wants to stay here.

SALLY: But she can't. You have to get her out. That's your job.

VEITCH: I'm not proud of it.

SALLY: What's the matter with you? You're brilliant at your job. You're a success.

VEITCH: We don't need this one.

SALLY: Does Murray know that? He's got a dangerous structure notice on this place, she has to get out by four o'clock today and you're wrecking the whole deal? Andrew?

VEITCH: Just one deal.

SALLY: Worth millions? He'll finish you. What about you and me? Our life together? All our plans for the house and our future? You've worked so hard for Golden Future Properties, don't throw it all away.

VEITCH: Sally...

SALLY: You can't go on with this. He'll kill you.

VEITCH: No he won't.

SALLY: He'll destroy us.

VEITCH: I haven't much time.

SALLY: Us, Andrew. Not just you. What you're doing is not just about you. It's about me as well and everything you ever promised me.

He looks at her.

Let the notice stand. I'll help her pack, take her to the hotel. I can make sure all the furniture's stored properly. Please, Andrew, don't ask for trouble.

VEITCH: I love you. And the life we've built together. But I'd love you anyway. I've always fought from the easy side, the side with power, the side with money and no conscience. Rode over them all, Sally, and told myself I was doing it for us and because 'business is what keeps this country on its fucking feet.' This time, Lester and his masses, Vollendorf, Collins, Northam Borough Council – they're all ranged against one little old lady and her house. And I'm fighting on her side, because this time it's worth fighting for, and, Sally, if we ever have those children we've got planned, they'll want a father who does the right thing, won't they? Won't that be better than a black japanned chest?

Beat.

SALLY: You won't be around to do any fathering if you carry on with this nonsense.

VEITCH: I have to…

He goes out. MISS BARWICK appears at the bottom of the stairs. She has changed into a pair of ancient overalls with an old colonial helmet on her head.

MISS BARWICK: Ready for action.

SALLY: Miss Barwick.

MISS BARWICK: Please call me Belle. And may I call you Sally? You look delightful in your hat.

SALLY: So do you. What are you going to do?

MISS BARWICK: I'm going to hold the ladder for Andrew.

Suddenly SALLY has to sit.

Are you all right?

SALLY: Yes. No. This is ridiculous. Andrew is risking his life, do you know that?

MISS BARWICK: Do you think so?

SALLY: Just because you're too selfish to move. This house is far too big for you...you don't know what Murray's like I...oh.

She doesn't feel well.

MISS BARWICK: You're pregnant aren't you?

SALLY: What?

MISS BARWICK: Just a guess.

SALLY: A bit sick.

MISS BARWICK: And Andrew doesn't know.

SALLY: Miss Barwick...

MISS BARWICK: Belle. Can I get you something to drink?

SALLY: No, I'm...no, thank you.

MISS BARWICK: Not used to it yet?

SALLY: I've only just found out.

MISS BARWICK: How very special you must feel.

SALLY: We're too busy. There's too much to do. It's not... I can't...go ahead...not now.

MISS BARWICK: Yes you can. Do you know how much your husband loves you? I'm 87. How many years do you think I have longed to have someone like Andrew to love me? To have a child of my own to hug and kiss? It wasn't a question of not now. It was a question of not ever. Do you think I would be here alone if I'd had a son or daughter to care for me? To fight for me? But I have Andrew. Your Andrew.

SALLY: He has to get you out of this house.

MISS BARWICK: He's going to save it for me.

SALLY: This site is worth a huge amount of money. Andrew's worked very hard to get this far – he deserves his share. He…had nothing, you know.

MISS BARWICK: Of course you deserve to be rich…have a lovely home.

SALLY: There's still so much to do.

MISS BARWICK: But you're already rich beyond compare, Sally, because your husband is one of the most courageous and loving men I have ever met. Give him the most important thing – a family – a wife who loves him unconditionally and a child to stand tall for. When I was little, I had a family. Now I have no one. Let it be the other way round for Andrew.

SALLY: But Murray…

MISS BARWICK: Your child needs parents who will stand up to the bullies of this world.

SALLY: You're like my grandmother.

MISS BARWICK: Is she still alive?

SALLY: Yes. She…likes to be hugged.

MISS BARWICK: So do I.

SALLY hugs her. SALLY touches her stomach.

SALLY: You won't tell him?

MISS BARWICK: That's your job.

Enter VEITCH.

VEITCH: Right, I'm going up. Be careful if you go out.

MISS BARWICK: I'm coming to hold the ladder.

SALLY: What do you want me to do?

VEITCH: What?

SALLY: I want to help. What do you want me to do?

VEITCH: Really?

SALLY: Really.

VEITCH: Phone the District Surveyor's office. Get one of the inspectors here for three o'clock. On no account speak to a man called Collins.

SALLY: I'll go round in person. I can use all my powers of persuasion then, and make sure we're back here on time.

VEITCH: You're a mate.

SALLY: I hope so.

VEITCH: OK let's go!

They all make for the door.

SCENE 3

Late Thursday afternoon. VEITCH, GILBEY, MISS BARWICK, and SALLY are drinking their second bottle of campari. All except SALLY are in dusty overalls.

VEITCH: We did it! We did it!

GILBEY: Not a bad job though I say it myself.

SALLY reads a document.

SALLY: *I have made an inspection at the above property on Thursday the 25 October and can find no adequate reason for continued enforcement of a dangerous structure notice.*

GILBEY: The poor bastard will no doubt get a bollocking, but it'll hold. They have to appear to operate within the law.

SALLY: Why are there three cars and a van parked nose to nose out there and an enormous pile of rubble on the pavement?

GILBEY: Protecting Crooked Wood against any lorries going astray and accidentally bumping into it.

VEITCH bangs the door and the light comes on.

MISS BARWICK: That's cosy. It's getting dark outside.

She draws the curtains.

GILBEY: I'll go and put our copy in a safe place.

He picks up the document.

VEITCH: Thanks Quentin.

GILBEY: You'll be looking for a job, Andy.

VEITCH: I'll survive.

GILBEY: Goodbye, dear lady.

He kisses MISS BARWICK's hand.

MISS BARWICK: But I owe you some money.

GILBEY: Just a few bags of cement. I'll send you the bill.

MISS BARWICK: Perhaps you would come back and do the stairs.

GILBEY: I'll organise it.

Exit GILBEY.

MISS BARWICK: I want to give you something.

VEITCH: There's no need.

MISS BARWICK: But I want to express my gratitude. They'd have come to take me away and goodness knows where I would have found myself. I might never have come home again. Is there something you'd like particularly? A piece of furniture, although I know you have a special house and it may not fit.

VEITCH: You must keep it all, Belle. You were entrusted with it.

MISS BARWICK: I know, the chest.

SALLY and VEITCH look at each other.

I know it needs some attention.

SALLY: It's very valuable.

MISS BARWICK: Please take it.

She kisses them both.

What I need now is a hot bath and a change of clothes.

VEITCH: Me too.

SALLY: Come back with us to the hotel. You can have a bath.

MISS BARWICK: I'm staying here. I'll boil a kettle.

VEITCH: I'm coming back to stay with you tonight, Belle. In
the meantime, don't answer the door to anyone, will you.

MISS BARWICK: I'll be all right.

VEITCH: Promise.

MISS BARWICK: Why don't you two go and have a bath
together?

*She grins at them and they leave. She shuts the door gently behind
them and the light behaves itself. She switches on one of the table
lamps. That behaves. She winds up the gramophone and puts on*
Who Stole My Heart Away. *She starts for the stairs. The lights
flicker. She pauses, then comes back for her torch.*

*There is a knock at the front door. She freezes. Another knock. The
record continues.*

There is a breaking of glass at the kitchen window. LESTER *is in.
The record comes to an end.*

LESTER: Miss Barwick? Miss Barwick?

MISS BARWICK: Who's that?

LESTER: I want to talk to you.

MISS BARWICK. What do you want? I haven't any money.
Who is it? Mr Murray.

LESTER: Murray *Lester!* Andrew Veitch has made a big
mistake, Miss Barwick. A big mistake.

MISS BARWICK: What mistake?

He comes towards her.

LESTER: Not getting you out of here on time.

MISS BARWICK: Stay there!

LESTER: There's nothing to be alarmed about. I couldn't make you hear the door, that's all.

MISS BARWICK: So you broke in through the kitchen window.

LESTER: Well that's not very difficult.

MISS BARWICK: How dare you!

LESTER: Such an old house.

MISS BARWICK: He's coming back.

LESTER: Who is?

MISS BARWICK: Mr Veitch.

LESTER: He has an appointment in Amsterdam. He's left you alone, Miss Barwick.

MISS BARWICK: No.

LESTER: I have a car outside. Will you collect your things?

MISS BARWICK: Why?

LESTER: You can't live here any more. It's unsafe.

MISS BARWICK: They've made it safe.

The document.

LESTER: Playing at builders, Miss Barwick. Playing you all along. Leaving you here in a house that is going to collapse any minute. You have to go. If you don't, you will find yourself under a pile of rubble. Your house is about to kill you, Miss Barwick.

MISS BARWICK: They've done another inspection.

LESTER: Don't believe them.

MISS BARWICK: I don't believe you.

LESTER: I'm not the one who came here pretending to mend the roof, pretending to mend the boiler, pretending to care about an old bird like you, when all the time he's making the holes bigger, knocking down the chimney.

MISS BARWICK: It had to come down.

LESTER: Lies, Miss Barwick! Can't you feel it shaking, this house? Trembling. Waiting to fall...? Where's Andrew now, eh? He'll come back tomorrow all shocked and amazed to find this house fallen down with you inside it. Business done. What he knocked on your door for in the first place – done.

MISS BARWICK: What you sent him to do in the first place! You corrupted that young man Mr Lester.

LESTER: What!

MISS BARWICK: When he came to work for you.

LESTER: He climbed the ladder of success in a thriving business.

MISS BARWICK: There are ways of getting rich that are good and honest, that give a person a sense of achievement; that make a person proud of his work, and loved by his community. That's what you could have done for Andrew.

LESTER: He was nothing before he met me.

MISS BARWICK: But no, you showed him the greedy grasping side of modern Britain; be bigger and better and richer than anyone else and share your fortune with no-one, lest they get bigger and better and richer than you.

LESTER: Some people, the clever people, have always got rich in this country

MISS BARWICK: But they've shared it! Look at all the towns and cities in the land with libraries and concert halls and art galleries that have been built by local boys made good wanting to put something back into their own communities. Now they don't even pay taxes because they squirrel it away in offshore banks. How satisfying is that?

LESTER: We're running out of time, Miss Barwick! Why don't you go and get your things before it's too late!

MISS BARWICK: How can you believe that Andrew is prepared to go to the lengths of killing an old lady who stands in the way of a huge property deal, unless that's what you too would do?

LESTER: I've come to rescue you.

MISS BARWICK: To get me out of the house so you can knock it down!

LESTER: I'll knock it down with you in it if you don't get out!

MISS BARWICK: You're a bully and a coward!

LESTER: It's the end of the road, Miss Barwick! Come on!

He grabs her arm.

MISS BARWICK: Phone Andrew!

LESTER: He's not your knight in shining armour! He works for me and he's on his way to Amsterdam organising a very big pay off…

Beat.

MISS BARWICK: All right. Could you get my bag. I packed some things. Upstairs. On my bed.

LESTER: About bloody time.

As he rushes up the stairs, the stairs give way, the lights go out and there is a sickening crash and thud as LESTER falls to the ground.

MISS BARWICK shines her torch into the dust and debris.

MISS BARWICK: Mr Murray, are you all right?

Silence.

Oh no…

Silence. She sings:

Oh God our help in ages past
Our hope for years to come
Our shelter from the stormy blast
And our eternal home

Her voice tails away.

SCENE 4

GILBEY arrives.

GILBEY: What happened?

VEITCH: Staircase gave way with Murray on it. Shock gave him a fatal heart attack.

GILBEY grimaces in sympathy.

GILBEY: And Miss Barwick?

VEITCH: Took her back to the hotel for the rest of the night but she insisted on returning here this morning. She's making coffee.

Enter MISS BARWICK from kitchen. She looks forlorn.

GILBEY: You warned everybody who was invited into the house. He was an intruder. You had no chance to warn him. The stairs were your self-defence.

MISS BARWICK: I sent him upstairs deliberately.

GILBEY: You didn't know he had a weak heart.

VEITCH: None of us knew that.

MISS BARWICK: But he died.

VEITCH: You could have died.

MISS BARWICK: All over a house.

VEITCH: Your house, not his.

MISS BARWICK: I didn't want him to die.

VEITCH: I know.

MISS BARWICK: Will I be arrested?

VEITCH: It was an accident.

She goes to look at the stairs.

MISS BARWICK: Will I get another dangerous structure notice?

GILBEY: The staircase isn't part of the structure. It's still a safe house.

MISS BARWICK: Can it be rebuilt?

GILBEY: We can use some of the original parts. It will look exactly the same.

MISS BARWICK: I don't want a different staircase.

GILBEY: You'll have to live on the ground floor for a week or two.

She returns to the kitchen.

Is it over then?

VEITCH: Vollendorf's taking his business elsewhere.

GILBEY: And you?

VEITCH: Got a rather ostentatious funeral to organise.

GILBEY: Then what?

VEITCH: I've got something in mind. Interested in working together again?

GILBEY: Only if it's houses.

VEITCH: It's houses.

GILBEY: Then I am.

VEITCH: I'll be in touch.

Enter MISS BARWICK with coffee.

GILBEY: Got to go, sorry.

MISS BARWICK: No coffee?

GILBEY: Another day.

MISS BARWICK: Really?

GILBEY: Really.

MISS BARWICK: Goodbye, Quentin.

Exit GILBEY. MISS BARWICK turns to VEITCH.

VEITCH: We'll oil the creaks, mend the leaks, fill the cracks. Replace the sash-cords, choose new wallpaper, polish the glass and paint the doors.

MISS BARWICK: Just like Daddy.

VEITCH: And we'll put in some gentle central heating to stop the books and photographs from getting damp.

MISS BARWICK: I like an open fire.

VEITCH: That too.

MISS BARWICK smiles happily.

Sally and I would like to visit you if we may.

MISS BARWICK: Like having a family.

VEITCH: Yes. Belle, I've got the most marvellous news. Sally is going to have a baby. I'm going to be a father.

MISS BARWICK: Well, what a wonderful surprise.

She kisses him.

Congratulations.

VEITCH: So you see, we'll have to make sure you're all cosy and warm if we're going to bring the baby to visit.

MISS BARWICK: But I can't afford any of it.

VEITCH: My company owns all the houses in this street. All boarded up at the moment. When we'd acquired Crooked Wood, we were going to knock them all down and build well never mind what we were going to build.

MISS BARWICK: And now?

VEITCH: I want to restore all the houses and allow people to buy them to live in again.

MISS BARWICK: Will families be able to afford them?

VEITCH: Quentin will see to that.

MISS BARWICK: Good.

VEITCH: Belle, I would like to make you an offer.

MISS BARWICK: Yes, Andrew?

VEITCH: My company would like to renovate your house, in its original style with modern facilities, at our expense, in order to have a model and show house for the new Keynes Road site. You would be consulted on every move, and would receive visitors only by appointment.

MISS BARWICK: How very exciting.

VEITCH: Once the thriving Keynes Road community is established, Crooked Wood will be all yours again.

MISS BARWICK: How will I maintain it?

VEITCH: There will be money in trust agreed by my company. Well? What do you think of my offer?

MISS BARWICK: Oh, I accept. Thank you. But on one condition.

VEITCH: What's that.

MISS BARWICK: You won't let those awful people who lived next door move back.

VEITCH: Miss Barwick!

MISS BARWICK: Oh and Andrew, do keep going with the do-it-yourself. The boiler wouldn't have exploded if I hadn't poked my stick in it. Accidentally, you understand…

She touches the bruise on her face and winces sweetly.

The End

www.ingramcontent.com/pod-product-compliance
Ingram Content Group UK Ltd.
Pitfield, Milton Keynes, MK11 3LW, UK
UKHW031252020325
455690UK00007B/73

9 781840 028799